ARMENIA TRAVEL GUIDE 2020

MARIA ASATRYAN

OPPIAN

Published by Oppian Press
Helsinki, Finland

© Oppian Press
All rights reserved

ISBN 978-951-877-177-0

CONTENTS

GET TO KNOW ARMENIA

ARMENIA IS A PLACE WHERE HOSPITALITY STILL MATTERS, AND where there is no such thing as a stranger, where the first words used by new found friends in introducing you to others is "our guest" and the second, "my brother" or "my sister". Whether you are a first time visitor or returning to visit family and friends, Armenia welcomes you with open arms.

Few people know that Armenia was the first country in the world to adopt Christianity as a state religion, in A.D. 301.

Christianity has played an immensely important role in the shaping of the Armenian people for over 1,700 years. And Armenia's ancient churches—massive, sprawling complexes of ruins nestled into the wildly green canyons and mountaintops of the countryside—are among the world's best preserved. Armenia's churches are not the only attraction of its countryside. The wildflower-dappled hills and valleys here are full of pagan temples like Garni, just outside Yerevan, and cobblestoned "spa towns" like Dilijan, nicknamed "Armenia's Switzerland."

You will find that a lot of tourists love coming to Armenia because of how beautiful and diverse this country is even despite its small geographical size. Armenia will bring you the longest ropeway in the world, the longest Zip-line in the world, absolutely delicious cuisine and most popular Armenian wine that is popular in the globe especially across Europe and US. You will love its ancient culture, hospitable people, live many amazing hikes, rich nature and wildlife. Backpackers can enjoy the thrill of exploring the unbeaten tracks while luxury seekers may find that they do indeed have many choices as well.

Geographical information

Armenia is a country of Transcaucasia, lying just south of the great mountain range of the Caucasus and fronting the northwestern extremity of Asia. It is bounded by Georgia on the north, Azerbaijan on the east, Iran on the south, and Turkey on the west. Contemporary Armenia is a fraction of the size of ancient Armenia. The capital is Yerevan (Erevan).

The highest point in Armenia is the Aragats mountain that is located 4,090 meters above the sea level. Aragats is also the highest point of the Lesser Caucasus.

Population

Armenia's population is estimated at 2.96 million, down from the 3.018 million confirmed during the 2011 census. The country's population ranking is 137th in the world. The country has a population density of 101 people per square kilometer (263/square mile). Armenia's largest city, Yerevan, has a population of approximately 1.2 million people. Yerevan is one of the world's oldest, continually inhabited cities in existence to this day. This area of Armenia is where it is speculated that Noah's Ark would have landed, by all research and accounts. Armenia is urbanizing at a rate of 0.5%, but has seen a population decrease by about 6% over the most recent 4 years.

Armenia has a large diaspora, with about 8 million Armenians living throughout the world. This is much larger than the current 3 million population of Armenia itself. The largest communities outside of Armenia are in Russia, Iran, France, the U.S., Canada, Syria, Lebanon and elsewhere.

Climate

Armenia is located in subtropics, however, because of the high-mountainous character the climate is rather dry continental with hot summers (average temperature +25 C) and cold winters (average temperature -6C). Climate of Armenia in other regions is markedly continental. Summer is dry and sunny, lasting from June to mid-September. Winter is short and quite cold with plenty of snow. In the mountains the average summer temperature ranges between +10 and +22°C, and in the winter temperatures range between +2 and -14 °C. In plain lands the average January temperature is -5 °C, and July temperature is +25 °C. Maximum amount of precipitations falls out in spring and beginning of summer.

The weather in different areas of Armenia differs significantly, though.

Each season in Armenia has its own unique color and flavor and summer is no exception. Summer days are long, hot, yet light in Armenia due to the exquisite topography of the country. The weather in mornings and evenings is perfect for exploration and adventurous activities, while the hot afternoons are perfect for leisure around the pool. So grab your hiking shoes, a camera and some sunscreen as summer Armenia offers the perfect balance between active and relaxing holidays.

Armenian Airports

Armenia has two international airports – **Zvartnots International Airport**, in the capital Yerevan, and **Shirak International Airport**, in the city of Gyumri.

Zvartnots International Airport acts as the main

international airport of Armenia. It's the busiest airport of the country. After Armenia declared independence from the Soviet Union, the airport was renovated in a futuristic style. The building of the airport isn't only modern and secure, but also architecturally stunning. The renovated Zvartnots proves the quality of the service and the flights.

Shirak International Airport is the second largest airport in Armenia. It's located not too far away from the center of Gyumri. The equipment and the system used by the airport are newly developed putting it ahead of other airports located in mountainous areas.

Zvartnots International Airport offers flights to and from more than 50 cities throughout the world, with direct flights to Yerevan, Armenia, by 23 international carriers.

Shirak International Airport offers direct flights only to Russia.

Getting to Armenia by Train

Another way to travel to Armenia is by a train. This can only be accomplished from Georgia. The trains are in a good condition: clean and secure. The service on the trains is great and most importantly the prices are very reasonable.

Georgia offers travel by train from the following cities:

- Tbilisi-Yerevan, year-round, is a 10-hour train ride.
- Batumi-Yerevan during the summer season, a 15-hour train ride.

Getting to Armenia by Car

Traveling to Armenia by a car allows for more freedom on your side. Whether you choose to drive the car yourself or hire a driver, there's nothing more fun than a road trip. You will have more flexibility than you would have on a train or a bus.

Getting to Armenia by Bus

Many travel companies offer big tour buses from Georgia and Iran. The prices are much lower compared to renting a car or traveling by a plane. If you're traveling alone, the road may get lonely, so taking a bus along with other tourists like you may prove to be much more fun.

Getting to Armenia by Trekking or Cycling

If you're experienced in traveling by foot or by bicycle, you'll be happy to know that there are no obstacles from Iran and Georgia. It won't take you long to pass the border as there are no special complicated procedures. You'll be done with the border procedure in around 20 minutes or less.

Armenian Culture and Traditions

Armenia has cultural treasures for just about everyone. Armenia is a land rich with cultural heritage and traditions. While some traditions date back thousands of years, like its people, they have evolved to befit the modern age and are still celebrated today. The culture of Armenia encompasses many elements that are based on the geography, language, faith, literature, architecture, dance, and music of the people.

The Armenian Language

"Armenian is the language to speak with God" these were the words of worldwide famous English poet George Byron.

The Armenian language is the national language of Armenians and the official language of Republic of Armenia and Artsakh. It is one of the oldest languages in the world and was originated in Armenian highland. The Armenian belongs to the Indo-European language tree and occupies an independent branch. Most of the Armenian ancient manuscripts (more than 17,000) were written in ancient Armenian and now are kept in Matenadaran(Yerevan). Interested in the Armenian language?

Here are some examples for you to try and will be useful for you when you will be in Armenia.

Barev (Բարև) - [barev] - Hi / Hello

Shnorhakalutyun(Շնորհակալություն) - [shnorhakalutiun] - Thank you

Tstesutyun (Ցտեսություն) - [tsetesutiun] - Good Bye

Khndrum em (Խնդրում եմ) - [khendroom em] - Please

Ayo(Այո) - [ayo] - Yes

Voch (Ոչ) - [voch] - No

Knereq (Կներեք) - [kenerek] - Sorry

Duq xosum eq angleren (Դուք խոսում ե՞ք անգլերեն) - [dook khosoom ek angleren] - Do you speek English

Inch arje (Ինչ արժե՞) - [eench arzhe] - How much is it?

ARMENIAN ART

THE ARMENIANS ARE ONE OF THE OLDEST NATIONS IN THE world and certainly, have rich cultural heredity gained from ancestors. They always appreciated the art; even in ancient centuries, they knew how to create beautiful monuments and how to decorate them.

The Armenian Theatre is considered to be one of the oldest theatres in the world. It was originated in the 1st millennium BC and the first Armenian professional theatre was originated in the Hellenic period and the first performances were in tragedy and comedy. According to the Historian Plutarch, Tigran the Great (Mets) built an amphitheater in Hellenic Style, in the capital Tigranakert, in 69 BC. The country boasts a State Academic Theatre of Opera and Ballet, several drama theatres, theatres for children, orchestras, a national dance company, and the Yerevan film studios, which produce feature, documentary, and science films. The traditional folk arts, especially singing, dancing, and artistic crafts, are popular. The 20th-century Armenian composer Aram Khachaturian achieved worldwide renown.

The Armenian Music is one of the most important parts of Armenian culture, which has embraced new forms of music in recent years, while maintaining traditional styles too. This is evidenced by the world-class Armenian Philharmonic Orchestra that performs at the beautifully refurbished Aram Khachaturian Concert Hall in the Yerevan Opera House, where one can also attend a full season of opera. In addition, several chamber ensembles are highly regarded for their musicianship, including the Komitas Quartet, Hover Chamber Choir, National Chamber Orchestra of Armenia and the Serenade Orchestra. Armenian music originated in the 2nd millennium BC. The first time it was mentioned in the works of the Armenian historians Movses Khorenatsi and Pavstos Buzand. In 1880's professional composers start to gather and develop ancient Armenian songs. They were Makar Yekmalian, Nikoghaios Tirgranian. The most important historical figure in Armenian history Komitas began his career at that time and changed the history of music Art. He was a teacher who left huge cultural heredity that is still being used in nowadays Armenian music.

The Armenian Dance heritage is one of the oldest, richest and most varied in the Near East. From the fifth to the third millennia B.C., in the higher regions of Armenia there are rock paintings of scenes of country dancing. These dances were probably accompanied by certain kinds of songs or musical instruments. The Armenian National dances include group, solo, couple and round dances.

There are many types of the dances, but the most widespread are

- Lorke
- Kochari
- Yarkhushta

- Berd

The Armenian Literature - Literature began in Armenia around 401 A.D, when Mesrop Mashtots created the Armenian alphabet. This event which took place in the 5th century is considered to be one of the most important turning points of Armenian Literature. Through the years the elements of literature have changed as the stories and myths were passed on through generations. Only a handful of fragments have survived from the most ancient Armenian literary tradition preceding the Christianization of Armenia in the early 4th century due to centuries of concerted effort by the Armenian Church to eradicate the "pagan tradition".

The Armenian Art - The National Art Gallery in Yerevan has more than 16,000 works that date back to the Middle Ages, which indicate Armenia's rich tales and stories of the times. It houses paintings by many European masters as well. The Modern Art Museum, the Children's Picture Gallery, and the Martiros Saryan Museum are only a few of the other noteworthy collections of fine art on display in Yerevan. Moreover, many private galleries are in operation, with many more opening every year, featuring rotating exhibits and sales.

The Armenian Architecture - Armenian architecture comprises architectural works with an aesthetic or historical connection to the Armenian people. The number of sacred monuments (churches, monasteries, chapels, shrines and Khachkars, or stone crosses) is truly mind-boggling. There are more than 5,000 churches, monasteries and chapels in Armenia, and over 20,000 Khachkars in the small territory of the Republic alone! It is difficult to situate this architectural style within precise geographical or chronological limits, but many of its monuments were created in the regions of historical Armenia, the Armenian Highlands. Armenian architecture, as it originates in an earthquake-prone region, tends to be built with this hazard in mind. Armenian buildings tend to be rather low-slung and thick-walled in design. Armenia has abundant resources of stone, and relatively few forests, so stone was nearly always used throughout for large buildings. Small buildings and most residential buildings were normally constructed of lighter materials, and hardly any early examples survive, as at the abandoned medieval capital of Ani. The stone used in buildings is typically quarried all at the same location, in order to give the structure a uniform color. In cases where different color stones are used, they are often intentionally contrasted in a striped or checkerboard pattern. Powder made out of ground stone of the same type was often applied along the joints of the tuff slabs to give buildings a seamless look. Unlike the Romans or Syrians who were building at the same time, Armenians never used wood or brick when building large structures.

Rug Making is the traditional branch of the Armenian Art and one of the symbols of the Armenian culture. This art was originated in the 3rd -4th millenniums BC. The evidence of which, are the working tools, appliances, the remains of the fabric and the remains of material which were found during the excavations. Though women historically dominated carpet-weaving in Armenian communities, several prominent carpet-weavers in Artsakh are known to have been men, and in some cases whole families took up the art.

This branch of culture became famous especially in the early medieval period, during the reign of Bagratuni. Still, in that time Armenian rugs were famous in international markets. The foreign historians (8th -12th) mentioned about the high quality of the Armenian rugs. Many ancient rugs were kept until today, the ancient one is the "Yerakhoran" rug (1202), "Guhar" (1680), and both of them have the Armenian inscription on them.

The Armenian rugs have colorful ornaments and square form. They are made of wool and thread and have different patterns and decorations. The most widespread pattern was the symbol of a dragon (which means power and eternity), eagle and the medallion. On each rug were written the date, event and the name of the maker. The main colors of the rugs are the red, blue and brown. Every region of Armenia had its own rugs and carpets with unique decoration and the ornaments.

The rugs are other characteristic feature of Armenian culture. Being one of the oldest nations Armenians made rugs still in ancient times. They were the main decoration of any house, the Armenians used them to cover floors, walls, and sofas even tables. Though it is the 21st century, Armenians still use the traditional rugs for decorating the houses. Armenian traditional rugs are rich in colors with different patterns, and designs.

Lacemaking in Armenia - Like laces, Armenian needle lace seems to be an obvious descendant of net making. Where laces adds decorative stitches to a net ground, Armenian needle lace involves making the net itself decorative. There is some archaeological evidence suggesting the use of lace in prehistoric Armenia and the prevalence of pre-Christian symbology in traditional designs would certainly suggest a pre-Christian root for this art form. In contrast to Europe where lace was the preserve of the nobility, in Armenia it decorated everything from traditional headscarves to lingerie. Thus lacemaking was part of many women's lives.

ARMENIAN CUISINE

Do you want to know which nation is the most hospitable? The answer is "Armenians», without a doubt. Armenian Cuisine is a poem, every line of which has a peculiar and unique scent. It includes a number of big and small secrets. Closest perhaps to Mediterranean dishes (and there is still lively debate over who was the first to wrap succulent pieces of spice meat into grape leaves, calling it dolma), Armenian food is one of the healthiest you'll eat.

Most important in Armenian cuisine is its freshness. Armenia's food is picked when ripe, not for delivery, and it is naturally grown, much of it organic. Harvested at the peak of season, Armenia's fruits and vegetables are a riot of tastes and fragrances, sun-sweetened to perfection.

Armenian cuisine consists of numerous kinds of vegetables and fruit, different sorts of herbs, cheese, meat and fish, wine and pastries. It is as ancient as the history of Armenia, a combination of different tastes and aromas. The food often has quite a distinct smell. Closely related to eastern and Mediterranean cuisine, various spices, vegetables, fish, and fruits combine to present unique dishes.

And the next time you sip a glass of wine or brandy, thank the first Armenian who discovered how to ferment Armenia's sweet grape, creating the nectar of the gods. Xenophon wrote of an intoxicating drink that 5th century BC Armenians served his troops, and they have been fermenting fruits ever since, including some excellent types of fruit based vodka.

Armenian vintages are gaining recognition in the wine world, but **Armenian Brandy** has been famous for over 100 years. In fact, Armenian brandy is the only non-French variety to earn the right to call itself cognac, after a famous blind taste test at the International Exhibition in Paris in 1900. In particular, Armenian cognac is renowned worldwide (winner of several awards), and was considered by the late British Prime Minister, Sir Winston Churchill, as his favorite. It has often been referred to as the food of today.

A very important aspect of the Armenian cuisine is the traditional bread called **Lavash**. If you are sitting at the Armenian table, the first thing that they would treat you is the bread. Even those Armenians who live very far from their native country, never forget about their bread lavash. Lavash is a very thin, easily rolled layer of dough approximately one-meter-high, which is baked on a hot wall of a stove-tondir (stove dugged in the ground), which is burned and heated by a dry vine bough.

In 2014, "Lavash, the preparation, meaning and appearance of traditional bread as an expression of culture in Armenia" was included in the UNESCO Representative List of the Intangible Cultural Heritage of Humanity.

The Armenian dishes are famous for their special taste and spicy flavors. The most popular dishes are made of meat. The most important and special dish of every Armenian table is the barbecue. It is made with pork, lamb, beef or chicken.

Basturma (long pieces of cured meat, covered with crust of bitter seasoning) and **sujukh** (flat meat sausages, spiced by various seasoning) are also very popular in Armenia.

The other traditional dish of Armenian cuisine is the famous **"Tolma" or "Dolma"**. There are more than 50 types of traditional Dolma. It is considered to be the second main dish in Armenian tables. It is made with cabbage leaves, or grape leaves, rice, minced meat and other species. They also use vegetables (pepper, eggplant, tomato) instead of cabbage leaves. They wrap the leaves around the minced meat and rice and cook it with olive oil.

The fish has its special place in Armenian cuisine. The locals like to make fish, especially **"Ishkhan"**, **"Taraph"** **"Sig"**. Besides that Armenians have a special festival; dedicated to fish. In that festival, each restaurant and private cooks present their own handmade fish. It takes part in Abovyan town, where everyone can participate in that festival, see how the cooks make fish and of course, the participants are being treated to delicious fish dishes.

The Armenian soup, **Khash**, also has its own, unique place in the Armenian cuisine. The name khash originates from the Armenian verb khashél (Armenian: խաշել), which means "to boil." The dish, initially called khashoy, is mentioned by a number of medieval Armenian authors, e.g. Grigor Magistros (11th century), Mkhitar Heratsi (12th century), Yesayi Nchetsi (13th century), etc.

The traditional soups have also their special place. **"Harissa"** is one of the tastiest hot meals in Armenian cuisine. It is made with chicken meat and wheat. Armenians have many kinds of soups and salads, especially for vegans. The special soup made with **"Aveluk"** is the popular dish in Armenia. The "Aveluk" is edible herb which has healthy feature. There is also a very tasty salad made with "Aveluk".

Besides all the delicious dishes, Armenians have delicious and sweet desserts that attract everyone. The traditional Armenian sweet cakes are **"Gata"** and **"Pakhlava"** which are the decoration of any Armenian traditional table.

The Armenian "Gata" is not only traditional dessert but also has a great importance in Armenian cuisine. Armenians say that "Gata is not a simple food, it decorates every festive table, has the meaning of the luck and success". Gata has a special round shape and with special symbols. They say that in ancient times the Armenian Grandmothers designed the Gata with the help of fork even with a cross which means they get rid of evil. Some people claim that Gata symbolizes the strength of the family.

The other popular dessert is the "Pakhlava"; it is layered pastry with chopped walnuts, syrup or honey. It has really delicious taste, especially when it serves with hot tea. The other sweet dessert of Armenian cuisine is the sweet **"Sujukh"** or Armenian Snickers. It is a special dessert made with walnuts, "Doshab", and sugar.

Dried fruits are another feature of cuisine. They are an inseparable part of every Armenian festive table. The Armenian women are always busy in summer just because they make different jams for the winter. The Armenian grandmothers make the tastiest jams with different fruits and berries.

The apricot is the national fruit. Since Roman times, the apricot was known as Prunus Armeniaca, literally translated as " Armenian Plum". The apricot also originated in Armenia, cultivated over 6000 years ago and exported to Rome around 100 BC. Other native varieties include the peach, almond, pomegranate and fig. The pomegranate, with its symbolic association with fertility represents that nation. According to encyclopedia.com. "A popular Armenian drink to this day is tan, a mixture of water and soured yogurt".

Wines as well as cheese occupy a particular page in culinary art. Roots of viticulture and winemaking in Armenia go back to the oldest times. It is confirmed by the cuneiform inscriptions in Urartu (an ancient state populated by Armenians). Wine cellars in Armenian houses were filled with aroma. There stood wide clay jars full of wine, grapes were dried for winter (which is popular in Armenia even nowadays), winter sorts of grapes, peaches, quinces and pears were piled on a thread and hung up. Nowadays numerous kinds of wine are produced in Armenia: "Malaga," "Kagor," Saperavi, pomegranate, Muscat, etc. **Matchar** (new grape wine) is very popular in Armenia. Combination of brightly shining sun of Ararat valley, fertile soil and pure water give the opportunity to create real works of art when producing wine and cognac. We offer you to try to cook some of the dishes, especially loved in Armenia, yourselves, in order to really appreciate all taste colorings of the Armenian cuisine.

BEST PLACES TO EAT ARMENIAN FOOD

Tavern Yerevan or "Pandok" was founded in 2006 and already 12 years serves the best of Armenian and Caucasian cuisine, of course with their unique receipts. Here you can find everything that connected with local cuisine, the chiefs use only fresh and high-quality products for their dishes. In this restaurant, you will feel at home due to tasty food and peaceful atmosphere.

Want to feel the city's taste and smell, Tavern Yerevan waits for you to prove that here you can taste the popular dishes of Armenian cuisine accompanied by the Armenian traditional music.

Cuisine : Armenian,Caucasian,

Address : Amiryan 5 Str, Paronyan 7 Str, Khorenatsi 29/2, Teryan 91 Str, Yerevan

Phone : + 374 10 545 545, +374 99 545 545(Amiryan Branch)

Working hours : 10:00 - 00:00

Email : info@pandokyerevan.com

Website : https://pandokyerevan.com/hy

Dolmama

Being situated in one of the oldest buildings of Yerevan, Dolmama restaurant was opened in 1998. The name of the restaurant came from the Armenian word "Dolma" (the Armenian national dish) and "Mama" (means Mommy). Mommy makes the best.

The specialty of the restaurant is Dolma. But creative and skillful cooks make not only the traditional recipes but also present the guests Dolma with interesting and unique recipes that you will taste just there.

The second popular dish of the restaurant is the traditional Armenian "Khashlama" (means stewed meat) but the making of this national dish also differs because they have a unique way of making it.

The other popular dish is the Easter Pilaf another tasty dish with dried fruit, sweet raisins, and nuts.

Here if you love wine, you are lucky, Dolmama has a wide variety of Armenian as well as, French, Argentinian, Australian and Italian wines.

You will feel the spirit of Armenia right from the doorsteps. Everything is home-like cozy and beautiful. You wouldn't want to leave the restaurant. Pay attention to the details of the interior; tablecloths, pictures on the wall, and fresh flowers on the tables.

By the way, during warm weather, you can enjoy the Armenian cuisine in the garden of the restaurant, under vineyards. This is what you need to try.

Cuisine : Armenian,

Address : 10 Pushkin Str., Yerevan

Phone : +374 10 56 13 54, +374 10 56 89 31

Working hours : 11:00 - 23:30

Email : info@dolmama.am

Website : http://www.dolmama.am

Anoush

If you search a perfect place for enjoyable and peaceful meetings, romantic dinners and family events Anoush restaurant welcomes everyone. The Anoush restaurant is situated in luxurious Republica hotel which is like a gallery, not an ordinary restaurant because it presents the history of culinary of the ancient Armenian and Western-Armenian.

The menu of the restaurant has unique dishes, salads and great creations of Chief Cook. Here you can find not only Armenian traditional dishes but also exclusive foods made of exclusive receipt.

During your dinner, you will enjoy the music which creates comfortable and relaxing atmosphere.

Anoush restaurant organizes different wine tastings with the stories of wine creation.

Cuisine : Armenian,

Address : Amiryan Str. 7/1, Yerevan

Phone : +374 11 990000

Working hours : 07:00 - 23:30

Email : info@republicahotel.am

Website : https://www.republicahotel.am/

Tsirani Garden-Restaurant

The history of Tsirani started when Tsaruk Pap (grandfather) opened a little canteen in his yard. That little canteen always was full of visitors. In a short period of time, his small restaurant became famous, even tables and set weren't enough for the customers and he often used the table and the set of his own house.

Then he built the biggest restaurant in the history of Arinj and called it "Poqrik Stepanos" (little) in honor of his grandchildren. Later the secret receipts of Tsaruk's family were used in the nowadays Tsirani restaurant. The founder of nowadays big restaurant complex is the son of the famous Tsaruk Pap.

Tsirani complex has 4 ha area which was built in the apricot garden. It has 61 wooden open-air small houses and 10 closed pavilions. The banquet hall can serve nearly 320 guests.

The menu presents all the traditional dishes of Armenian national cuisine. A visit to this place is a real miracle in autumn when the leaves are yellow, the garden also has an artificial waterfall, a man-made lake and also a cave where you can have a dinner.

Cuisine : Armenian,

Address : Babajanyan block,3th Str. Arinj

Phone : +374 55 850 950, +374 99 850 950

Working hours : 09:00 - 02:00

Email : support@tsiranicomplex.am

Website : https://tsiranicomplex.am/

Lavash

Want to have traditional Armenian breakfast and unforgettable memories? Lavash restaurant offers the best dishes and Armenian sandwiches.

In one of the luxurious streets of Yerevan is located a nice restaurant which presents the cuisine of Armenia in a fresh and new way. The name of the restaurant is Lavash (a type of bread that has a completely Armenian origin). The aim of the founders was to create a harmonic unique atmosphere with special design and Armenian cuisine.

Lavash restaurant aims to bring back the forgotten Armenian "Brduchayin" (Armenian sandwich) breakfast and develop the culture of right morning breakfast. The menu of the restaurant includes not only the local cuisine but also popular dishes in a unique way.

If you want to eat right Armenian breakfast, this restaurant offers the best types of dishes and of course the popular Armenian Brduch.

Cuisine : Armenian,

Address : Tumanyan 21,Yerevan

Phone : +374 10 608 800, +374 91 608 800

Working hours : 09:30- 00:00

Website : https://lavash.restaurant/hy/

· · ·

Genacvale Pandok

Genacvale Pandok many years enjoys the locals' love and trust. The tavern has different branches in Yerevan city.

Genacvale tavern or pandok was founded in 2006. during eight years the restaurant managed to have different branches in Yerevan city. In 2016 was opened a new branch of the restaurant at Isahakyan Str. In front of every restaurant Kinto(Georgian trader) Geno welcomes everyone. Genacvale restaurant presents the Georgian cuisine with the popular dishes and of course with Georgian recipes.

In the tavern, you will feel the atmosphere of the Old Tbilisi, lovely music with the Armenian and Georgian instruments.

Cuisine : Caucasian,Georgian,

Address : Isahakyan 12,Yerevan

Phone : +374 10 277 999

Working hours : 10:00- 24:00

Email : info@genacvale.am

Website : https://www.genacvale.am/

Malkhas Jazz Club

Want to have the unforgettable evening with tasty food and fantastic jazz sounds, Malkhas Jazz club every day opens its doors to everyone.

Malkhas Jazz Club was founded by the Armenian great Maestro Levon Malkhasyan in 2006. Tasty food, great atmosphere, and excellent Jazz music wait for you in this club. Every day from 21:00 till 02:00 you can enjoy the program of Jazz music.

Cuisine : Armenian,

Address : Pushkin 52/1 Str, Yerevan

Phone : +374 10 535 350

Working hours : 21:00 - 02:00

Email : malkhasjazz@mail.ru

Where to taste best Coffee in Yerevan

For coffee addicts, Yerevan is an ideal place; coffee for Armenians is more than an invigorating drink. This is a whole ceremony: friends and family do love to gather and discuss business or just talk with a cup of coffee. No wonder why there are so many cosy coffee shops in Yerevan. If you are also a coffee addict and you want to taste good coffee in Yerevan, we suggest you to visit one of these coffee shops in Yerevan.

Malocco Cafe

Malocco is not just a place to have a cup of coffee, it's one of the coziest cafes in the city center that takes you to another century. Vintage interior and soothing music is tuned to a positive. In the menu you will find a great variety of coffee starting with a classic espresso and ending with branded coffee from Malocco. In addition, here you can taste delicious dishes of continental cuisine and spend an evening with a glass of wine.

Kitchen: Continental

Address: Tumanyan st 40, Tamanyan st 1, Yerevan

Phone: +374 99 53 13 27, +374 96 53 13 27

Working hours: 10:00-00:00

Segafredo Zanetti Espresso Yerevan

If you are familiar with Café Segafredo, you will certainly enjoy the idea of spending time in Segafredo Zanetti Espresso Yerevan. This is definitely the best place for true connoisseurs of coffee. The atmosphere, professional service, and, of course, unique coffee make Segafredo one of the most popular coffee shops in Yerevan.

Kitchen: Continental

Address: Amiryan st 3/37, North Avenue 1/5, Yerevan

Phone: +374 94 53 98 90, +374 93 54 52 06, +374 77 56 60 16

Working hours: 08:30-02:00

Coffeestory

There is nothing better than a cup of hot coffee in one of the city's most beautiful cafes. Coffeestory is a story in one cup, and each story is unique. The interior of the cafe is completed with interesting inscriptions that will take your attention while the barista makes the best coffee for you.

Kitchen: European, Continental

Address: Nalbandyan st 98/9, Yerevan

Phone: +374 11 44 00 00

Working hours: 10:00 – 0:00

· · ·

Coffeeshop Company Yerevan

Coffeeshop is part of the Coffeeshop Company brand in Yerevan, which managed to gain popularity across Europe and has already become one of the most beloved places in Yerevan. Professional barista, with the secrets of making the best coffee, will certainly surprise you.

Do you love tea? Coffeeshop has a separate line "Art of tea", where you can enjoy unique tea species, as well as buy a favorite variety.

Coffeeshop is a place where you can have lunch and hold a business meeting with a cup of the best coffee in the city.

Kitchen: Austrian, European, Snack menu

Address: Amiryan st 4/5, Yerevan

Phone: + 374 11 26 33 33, + 374 99 26 33 33, +374 11 27 33 33

Working hours: 08:30 – 02:00

Jazzve

Coffee served in a vintage jezve is one of the Jazzve cafe chips. In fact, the cafe was one of the first in the city, which presented the coffee house in a new format. Jazz, good coffee, nice atmosphere immediately pleased the locals and guests. Today, the cafe already has three branches.

Kitchen: Continental

Address: Tumanyan st 35, Abovyan st 2, Teryan st 83, Komitas 16, Arshakunyats 34/3, Yerevan

Phone:+374 10 53 20 48

. . .

Crumbs the Bread Factory

Crumbs cafe and bakery is a cozy place where it is always warm and the smells of delicious pastries is in the air. The bakery is specialized in baking bread and bakery products using only natural and environmentally friendly products. What could be better in cold weather than a cup of hot tea or coffee with delicious eclair. In addition, you will enjoy a pleasant atmosphere, a cozy interior and professional service in Crumbs the Bread Factory.

Address: Mashtots ave 37, Bayron 6 Yerevan

Phone:+374 10 537013, +374 10 703007, +374 10 546424

Working hours: 08:30-24:00

Lounge Bars of Armenia

You will always find something to do in Yerevan. The pink city has numerous restaurants, lounge bars and pubs where tourists can pass their evenings, relax, eat tasty dishes and of course have fun.

EL Sky Bar

EL Sky Bar is located on the rooftop of the Yerevan Plaza building. If you enjoy panoramic views of a gorgeous city while drinking a favorite beverage and listening to music. The white design of the bar and elegant attention to service makes you feel actually on top of the world.

Eden Café

Eden Café is located near the Cascade complex in the heart of Yerevan. You can enjoy the beautiful view of the Cascade in an outdoor cafe and there is also an underground hall where you can dance and have fun.

In Vino

In Vino is the first wine club, merchant and bar in Armenia. We love wine. We make wine in Armenia and in France. You'll enjoy your time at In Vino. They offer more than 850 wines from Armenia and all over the world. In Vino is the home of the famous baguette sandwiches, which are sold by centimeter. You tell us how many centimeters you are hungry for and we'll make the sandwich with a crispy French baguette right in front of you. You can enjoy it with a glass of wine or a freshly made espresso or tea.

Shopping in Armenia

In recent years, lots of shops, malls, department stores and markets have been built in Armenia, where anyone can find clothes, souvenirs and other things for any taste and possibilities.

Dalma Garden Mall

Dalma Mall is a two-storied shopping and entertainment complex, which is located near the center of Yerevan at Tsitsernakaberd Highway 3. This spacious and prestigious center is suitable for anyone who prefers civilian and comfortable shopping. For those who want to have a little rest there are cafeterias, pizzerias, as well as cinemas and bowling. Children also will not be bored, because a beautiful playground and a room for mother and children operate here.

Yerevan Mall

The complex is famous for its unique architectural design developed by world-renowned international companies "Broadway Malyan" and "Archangel". Here you will find a variety of designer shops, as well as a wide variety of entertainment choices. You can find Yerevan Mall at Arshakunyats ave. 34/3.

Rio Galleria

"Rio Galleria" shop plays a key role in the fashion business of Armenia. It presents collections from the first fashion houses and collaborates with world-renowned fashion designers. As it is common throughout the world, the collection here is updated each season and is brought just in time, before the start of a new season. You can find Rio Galleria at Northern ave. 8.

Rio Mall

"RIO" Yerevan offers its guests a high quality of service, as well as a wide range of goods and services. The shopping center is located at Vahram Papazyan St.

ARMENIAN TRADITIONS

Armenia is a warm and rich country, and Armenian traditions are no exception. From welcoming guests to celebrating life, Armenia's traditions make this country a wonderful place to visit. Before you visit, it's well worth it to read up on the traditions of Armenia so you know better what to expect and to give you context for all you'll see. While you may not attend a childbirth or wedding, you'll be sure to see some traditional Armenian clothing and houses, and a real highlight of any trip is Armenian hospitality.

Weddings

Armenian wedding is a very big holiday. The ceremony includes betrothal, engagement and wedding itself. The tradition of "seven days seven nights" celebration has become obsolete. The abundance of guests at Armenian wedding is a must. The so-called "God family" act as witnesses.

Wedding is accompanied by a number of various cheerful ceremonies. During the redemption of the bride any amount of money can be asked, and it's a matter of Godfather's honor to find this money; the sums are symbolical, though. The bride is taken to the altar by her sponsor and God family bear responsibility for the new family from the very beginning to end. At the wedding the bride is given a boy to cuddle – it is desirable that first-born is a boy. Next morning after the wedding women related to the groom bring a red apple symbolizing the virginity to the bride's home.

Birth of Child

Traditionally (especially in rural areas) Armenian families have a lot of children. A birth of a child, especially a boy, is a happy event which has always been welcome. On church holidays in front of the house where a baby was born music played and the house was decorated with green branches – the symbol of family continuation. The child is not shown to anybody but the relatives for 40 days after birth.

It is accepted that a person having any happy life occasion puts his hand on a head of his friend or relative saying "tarose kes" ("I pass it to you")- wishing them the same good luck.

Armenian National Clothing

Each nation has its values and national clothing is one of the values and an integral part of the history of the nation. Armenia, as one of the most ancient countries with a rich history has its own traditional clothing. Moreover, each province had its own unique style of clothing with distinctive embroidery and details. **Taraz**, Armenian national clothing is a pride of the Armenian nation, which has its unique place in the culture of Armenia. Alongside with learning the history of Armenian culture the history of Taraz is needed to be learnt.

Classic women taraz is a free wide dress with jag in the middle and on the sides. The main colors Taraz are black as a symbol of the earth, white – a symbol of water, red – the air, yellow – the symbol of flame. National clothing was a symbol of belonging to a particular class. The clothing could also determine whether the woman is married or how many children she had. Depending on the social status, woman's dress could be decorated with gold or silver threads. Women's dresses were made of satin, plush, silk and brocade.

The male costume consisted of a shirt and wide trousers. Collar shirt was decorated with embroidery. Shirt was made of cotton fabric or of goat fur. Style and color of coats varied depending on the province. Kaftan had fitted shape with narrow sleeves and a high collar. Men of high society wore light colored coats, men with lower status wore garments of dark tones. Western Armenians wore a vest with jacket over Kaftan.

Men's trousers were narrow shape at the ankles to make them feel comfortable while working on the field. At the waist trousers had wrapped wide scarf. Scarf has served not only as a belt but also as a pocket; in scarf layers men carried wallet and a knife.

In winter men wore sheepskin coats or vests made of goat fur.

The most important part of the national costume was the headwear for women and men. Men wore fur, woven and knitted hats. Depending on the province hats had tall and narrow form. Citizens wore cylindrical caps of Persial lamb.

Female headwear was more complex and diverse. The style

depended on the social status, whether a woman was married or not married. The main part of the headwear was a kind of a small turret, the handkerchief was tied over the turret. Scarf covered neck and lower part of face. Headwear was removed only if there was no man in the house.

Women of high society wore headbands adorned with precious stones, gold and silver.

National costume was completed with handmade shoes, which were called threkh. Best shoes were made of rough skin, worn with woolen socks. Women's shoes were backless and of acute form. Citizens wore boots with high heels and long curved toes. Urban ladies wore leather boots with soft soles.

Taraz is a very colorful costume, but, unfortunately, you can hardly see anyone wearing national costume on the street. Or you can see all the beauty of national costumes worn by dancers. You can also see unique collection of national costumes of different Armenian provinces in the National History Museum in Yerevan.

NATIONAL HOLIDAYS

ARMENIA'S HOLIDAYS ARE A MIX OF OLD TRADITIONS DATING back to pagan times, Christian religious holidays, and modern additions. Some holidays are international, like New Year's and International Women's Day, and can be celebrated in Armenia and around the world. Some holidays show off Armenia's local traditions, like Vardavar and Terendez. And even though they're much newer, holidays like Victory Day and Republic Day tell a lot about Armenia's recent history. Holidays in Armenia are a great way to experience a bit of local culture yourself and take your trip to Armenia to the next level.

Vardavar

In Armenia, there are few holidays, covered with such spirit of mischief and childishness, as Vardavar. Despite its serious origin (a holiday is the church one, and it is called the Transfiguration of the Lord), Vardavar is considered the funny and amusing holiday, because the main rite of this day is the sprinkling water on everything and everyone! Young and old, rich and poor poured water on each other, at that not resisting and not offending at all! Vardavar is celebrated 98 days after Easter and always falls on hot summer months. Therefore, dousing is more than urgently at this time. Especially that according to legend, the water is endowed with healing power on this day.

The history of this funny custom is in the pagan roots of ancient Armenia and is connected with the two legends. According to the first legend, the goddess of love and beauty Astghik poured everyone with the rose-water, spreading the love. The second parable says, the holiday occurred in the honor of victory over evil rich man, who prohibited people to use water. Hence the "vard" means "water"," var" means "to wash with water". Also on this day it is customary to cook meals and visit relatives and friends.

SAFETY IN ARMENIA

ARMENIA IS ONE OF THE SAFEST COUNTRIES IN THE REGION. Health precautions are minimal; just exercise the same type of caution you would if travelling in Europe. The country is provided with safe and clean water. Here you can drink water straight from the water tap without fear for your health; however, it is not only safe, but also delicious, as it comes from mountain springs. You can also find little fountains ("pulpulak") where you can drink water for free. Outside Yerevan, it's probably wise to avoid drinking tap water.

Many Armenians drive erratically, overtaking in the face of oncoming traffic and on blind corners, speeding and taking no notice of delineated road lanes. When driving, stay alert and drive extremely defensively.

Armenia is a country with a low crime rate. You can safely move around the city, go to public places and use public transport, as the country has very low statistics on street crime, pickpocketing, and theft. It is also important to note that unlike many other countries, where late hours are considered unsafe, in Armenia you can safely walk even late at night. There is an interesting explanation of this phenomenon: Armenia is a small country, where 96% of the population are Armenians, that's why any kind of crime is quickly determined, and the guilty are punished.

In 2015, the Gallup Law and Order Index revealed the countries in which people feel the safest to walk home alone at night. Armenia is placed 9th in the list. The index is a worldwide measure of people's sense of personal security in local areas, as well as their own experiences with law enforcement. The report is based on more than 142,000 interviews with adults in 141 countries in 2014.

However, despite these favorable indicators, minimal amounts of crime do exist in the country. Therefore, tourists are always advised to follow basic personal safety measures: not to leave their belongings or valuables unattended and follow all the necessary instructions while visiting museums, theaters, and other public places.

It is also important to note that you should be very careful when you take a taxi outside the airport. Some taxi drivers can approach to you and offer to take you to the right place, however at the end, they may cheat and ask a fee in excess of the required amount. That's why it's better to take a state taxi provided by the airport. If you want to know which one is a real taxi, just look at the number plate: if it is yellow or the first are 3 digit numbers than it is a taxi you can take. And keep in mind that on almost every taxi the first 5 km cost 600 AMD, and then each additional kilometer is 100 drams.

Recently, one of the famous international newspapers has made a rating of the terrorist attack possibilities around the world, and Armenia occurred in the last places. And indeed: our country can be considered one of the safest countries in terms of the threat of terrorism. That fact is easily explained: as it was already mentioned above, Armenia is a mononational country where 96% of the population are Armenians, professing the Christian religion. For this reason, a peaceful atmosphere reigns in the country, and there is a complete absence of both ethnic and religious hatred.

Armenians are peaceful and good-natured people. You can very rarely witness fights or drunken fracases on the streets. And, probably, it's not a coincidence that there have never been sobering-up stations in the country.

The capital is also staffed by special police units, called "guardian angels." They keep watch in the country, and you can appeal to them on any issue. In case of need, every one of them is carrying a first aid kit.

PUBLIC TRANSPORTATION

PUBLIC TRANSPORTATION IN YEREVAN IS COMPOSED MOSTLY OF small and large buses, trolley buses, as well as a metro line. All trips cost 100 AMD.

Smaller white buses called **marshrutkas** are the most common form of public transportation and they go to every part of the city. Larger buses serve more frequently traveled routes.

There are also buses and electric trolleybuses following numbered routes. Tickets cost AMD 100.

The Yerevan metro is clean, safe and efficient. It runs north–south through the city, stopping at these underground stations: Barekamutyun, Marshall Baghramyan, Yeritasardakan, Republic Square (Hanrapetutyan Hraparak), Zoravar Andranik near Surp Grigor Lusavorich Cathedral/Rossiya Mall and Sasuntsi Davit at the Yerevan train station. The line continues west and south on ground level to stations in the industrial suburbs. Trains run every five to 10 minutes between 6.30am and 11pm and one-way tickets cost AMD100.

Taxis are cheap and plentiful, and range from well-loved Ladas to late-model Benzes. There are two types: street taxis and telephone or call taxis. Prices are AMD600 for the first 5km and then AMD100 per kilometer. Make sure the driver switches the meter on or you may be overcharged. A great option is the **GG Taxi service**, the Armenian analogue of Uber. If you are running an Android or IOS device, just download the GG taxi app from the application store, sign up with your phone number and order cabs by a tap or two. The app offers various types of transportation, including XL size for larger groups.

What you need to know about public transportation in Armenia

- The public transportation in Yerevan costs only 100 AMD (0.25$). It's a fixed price for buses and minibuses and the price doesn't change depending on the distance of your ride. There are no tickets and you pay directly to the driver. Prices for transportation from Yerevan to other areas of the country varies from 200AMD to 7000AMD, depending on the distance.
- All the signs and names of the bus stops and areas on city buses and marshrutkas are in Armenian.
- No free seats doesn't mean no space at all. Picking up passengers who will simply stand in the minibus is very common. Drivers usually pick up as many passengers as they can squeeze in their vehicles. Note that this doesn't apply to long-distance trips outside Yerevan.
- There are no buttons to signal the driver that you

need to get off. You will have to tell the driver to stop, hoping he did hear you.

- Marshrutkas are wonderful for socializing. People engage in conversations, ask each other to pass the money to the driver, pass the change back etc.

Additional Tips

Here is some useful information on how to get to cities around Armenia from different bus stations.

Kilikia Central Bus Station: Ashtarak, Oshakan, Ohanavan, Agarak, Talin, Byurakan, Etchmiadzin, Armavir, Stepanavan, Alaverdi, Sisisan, Jermuk, Stepanakert (Artsakh). Minibuses to Tbilisi as well as buses to Tehran also depart from the Kilikia Central Bus station.

Call center's phone number: +374 10 565 370 (Please, note that they might not be able to answer in English).

Northern Bus Station: Sevan, Dilijan, Ijevan, Chambarak, Martuni, Gavar, Vardenis

Call center's phone number: +374 10 621 670 (Please, note that they might not be able to answer in English).

Sasuntsi David Station: Ararat, Vedi, Khor Virap, Yeghegnadzor

Gai Bus Station: Buses to Garni (Garni pagan temple and Geghard monastery)

P.S. Please, note that the list is incomplete and the bus station destinations are changing frequently.

ACCOMMODATION

IF YOU HAVE NEVER BEEN TO YEREVAN BEFORE, CHOOSING THE right accommodation may be a challenging task. There is a big choice of hotels, hostels and apartment rentals in Yerevan and each of those properties offers various deals and promotions, so it may become difficult to make the right choice.

Before starting your research, you need to understand what factors are the most important for your trip. Do you want to stay close to main attractions so that you won't have to use public transport? Or maybe you are traveling on business and high-speed internet and comfortable meeting rooms are your priority? These questions will help you narrow down the list of Yerevan hotels to the most relevant ones.

Location of Yerevan Hotels

Just like anywhere else in the world, most of Yerevan attractions are located in the city center. So if your primary purpose of visit is tourism, then it makes sense to choose one of the following options: hotels located near

Republic Square or near the Opera House. From these 2 main areas you will be in a walking distance from such Yerevan sights as the Cascade, Matenadaran, History Museum of Armenia, the Northern Avenue, etc.

Facilities and Services

Depending on the purpose and time of your visit, you may need different amenities in a hotel. If you are traveling to Yerevan in summer, it would be nice to have an outdoor pool at the hotel, because the summers tend to be quite hot in Armenia. Another thing to look for is a high quality internet connection. While most of the hotels in Yerevan offer free WiFi, not all of them have it in the rooms. Free airport transfer is also something that you may need when traveling to Yerevan.

Prices of Yerevan Hotels

Hotels in Yerevan range from low budget comfort type to upscale 5 star hotels, so there is a hotel for every budget. But **when** choosing a hotel, you need to consider the actual value for money and free-of charge services included in the price. It also makes sense to visit the hotel website for special offers, package deals and promotions.

Reviews and guest comments

When you have a shortlist of Yerevan hotels, it's time to look at the reviews. Nowadays customer feedback can tell much more about the hotel than all of the information and photos combined. You can read traveler reviews on Tripadvisor, as well as booking engines like Booking.com and Expedia.com.

Since different travelers have different needs and

expectations, it's good to sort the reviews by traveler type (solo, family, business, etc).

Here's the list of some of the best hotels you can stay in Yerevan, for all your sightseeing needs.

Hyatt Place Yerevan Hotel

This hotel is a great, clean-cut option (with a large number of amenities) located in the center of Yerevan. A favorite for business people and conference goers, Hyatt Place is sleek, modern, and incredibly comfortable. Guests have access to a fitness center, various dining options, and bars, and can take advantage of the hotel's proximity to Yerevan's numerous restaurants and shops.

26/1 Vazgen Sargsyan Street, Yerevan, Armenia

Tel.: +37411221231

DoubleTree by Hilton Hotel Yerevan City Centre

DoubleTree by Hilton is situated near the Republic Square and boasts a spa and wellness center, fitness room, and a sauna, making it an ideal place to indulge and relax in after a long day in the city. The rooms are well-furnished with a seating area, beautiful views of Mountain Ararat, and a free minibar, along with other necessary items like comfy bathrobes, slippers, and a hairdryer.

4/2 Grigor Lusavorich Street, Yerevan, Armenia

Tel.:+37411555333

· · ·

Europe Hotel

Located just 500 meters from the gorgeous Sourp Krikor Lusavorich Cathedral, the hotel offers rooms with modern décor, minibars, cable TV and air conditioning. Europe Hotel is a great option for those who like to be in the center of things and close to the city's attractions, but are also looking for a peaceful and comfortable stay.

38 Hanrapetutyan Str, Yerevan, Armenia

Tel.: +37410546060

Marriott Yerevan

Located right in the center of Republic Square, referred to by locals as the Hraparak, this hotel is easily one of the best choices for staying in Yerevan. The Marriott is famed for attracting a wide range of guests, from tourists, businesspeople traveling for work, and even the Kardashian family, and all for good reason. Sit outside on the patio and watch all of Yerevan go by, from newlyweds circling the Square in decorated limousines (a local custom) to street vendors selling figs and berries and, of course, the gorgeous fountain shows that take place in the evening.

1 Amiryan Street, Yerevan, Armenia

Tel.: +37410598997

Paris Hotel Yerevan

This boutique hotel, located in downtown Yerevan, has the perfect touch of French-inspired chic. The lobby's décor consists of creamy whites and soothing neutrals, similar to that of a trendy Parisian home, the guest rooms are equally as inviting, both in comfort and design, and there is delicious French cuisine offered at breakfast, lunch, and dinner. On warm evenings, guests can head up to the rooftop restaurant and bar to watch the sun as it sets over Yerevan.

4/6 Amiryan St., Yerevan, Armenia

+37410602997

Best Western Congress Hotel

The Best Western Congress Hotel is especially good for families and large groups. The amenities at this hotel make for a comfortable and hospitable stay, and there is a fitness center for health-conscious guests, as well as a Russian sauna to help you unwind after a long day of exploring. Unlike many other hotels in Yerevan, the Congress Hotel has a large swimming pool.

1 Italy Street, Yerevan, Armenia

+37410591199

Nova Hotel Yerevan

This very centrally located hotel boasts modern design and bright colors. All the important landmarks are close by, including the Opera and Ballet Theater and Republic Square. There is a kettle in every room for an invigorating cup of tea at any time of the day, while many of the rooms also have comfortable sofas and armchairs for a relaxing stay.

10/5 Sayat Nova Avenue, Yerevan, Armenia

Tel.: +37410600050

. . .

Ani Plaza Hotel

Ani Plaza Hotel features an indoor swimming pool, sauna, and gym. Located in the entertainment and business district of the city, this 4-star hotel is within walking distance of Republic Square, the Opera House, Cascade, and the National Gallery. Rooms at the hotel feature cozy carpets, warm colors, and air conditioning, and some even have panoramic views of Mount Ararat and Yerevan.

19 Sayat Nova Avenue, Yerevan, Armenia

Tel.: +37410589500

Hotel National

Hotel National is a luxurious lodging option for tourists who want to experience a comfortable stay at a trendy boutique hotel. Republic Square is only a three-minute walk away and guests can still get the relaxation they need through the hotel's amenities, which include an equipped fitness center and a beautiful indoor pool, as well as a gorgeous lounge to hang out in. There is also an excellent on site restaurant and bar, which has received rave reviews from guests.

4/3 Amiryan Street, Yerevan, Armenia

North Avenue Hotel

Northern Avenue, which is less than a decade old, is rapidly becoming the Rodeo Drive or Fifth Avenue of Yerevan, featuring luxury designer stores, boutiques, and restaurants. This hotel is situated right on the avenue and makes for a perfect stay in the middle of a new and developing portion of an old city. The North Avenue Hotel is designed with a sleek, modern touch, and features an eclectic winding staircase. Be sure to dine at La Perla, the hotel's Spanish restaurant, which has received praise for its Mediterranean cuisine as well as for its impressive wine inventory.

10/1 Northern Avenue, Yerevan, Armenia

Tel.: +37410505055

Holiday Inn Express Yerevan Hotel

Holiday Inn Express Yerevan is located in the city center near the newly opened park of Mashtots. Sightseeing of Yerevan such as Republic square, Theater of Opera and Ballet, Museum of history are situated in 5 minutes within walking distance to the hotel.

Holiday Inn Express Yerevan has 15 floors and offers 130 comfortable standard double or twin rooms to its guests.

97/2 P. Buzand street, Yerevan, Armenia

Tel.: (+374) 10 25 31 41

Opera Suite Hotel

Opera Suite Hotel was awarded 4-star hotel category.

The hotel is situated very close to the Opera House, within 1.5 km distance from the Republic Square and very close to Baghramyan Metro Station.

The hotel features open air swimming pool, indoor swimming pool, sauna, fitness center, SPA center, massage salon, beauty salon as well as lobby bar, restaurant, sky bar, open air café, business center and conference halls.

It's offering to its guests comfortable furnished deluxe, suite and executive rooms as well as non-smoking rooms. All rooms feature air conditioning, a seating area, flat-screen TV with satellite channels and free Wi-Fi. The kitchenettes are equipped with a fridge, stove and electric kettle. The bathrooms come with a hairdryer, bathrobes and slippers.

1 Baghramyan Str. 1-3, Yerevan, Armenia

Tel.: (+374) 10 25 31 41

CURRENCY AND PRICES IN ARMENIA

One of the reasons why tourists prefer to spend their holiday in Armenia is very affordable prices. Below we will acquaint you with the prices for various goods and services in Armenia so that you can feel comfortable after your arrival.

Every traveler while planning a vacation, often wonders in what currency it is most advantageous to take cash when traveling, and whether it is necessary to take the money in cash or use a credit card?

Currency Exchange in Armenia: Armenian National Currency

For nearly two decades, to be more exact, since 1993, after the collapse of the Soviet Union and the independence as "Armenian Dram" has become the national currency having replaced the Soviet ruble. National currency and all "financial issues" of Armenia are regulated by the Central Bank of Armenia. It is worth noting that AMD is the national currency not only of the Republic of Armenia, but also of

Artsakh, which has been inhabited by native Armenians for millennia. So if you are planning to visit the ancient Artsakh, the problems with the currency will not arise.

Dram in Armenian language means money, but the word has Greek roots. In international format, the Armenian dram is denoted as **AMD**. Currently in circulation are banknotes with the nominal value of 1000, 2000, 5000, 10 000, 20 000 and 100 000 AMD, as well as coins in denominations of 10, 20, 50, 100, 200 and 500 drams.

On the AMD banknotes are represented prominent figures of culture, which had a great contribution to the history and spiritual development of the country; historically valuable monuments and beautiful fragments of the paintings of the great Armenian painter Martiros Sarian.

In Armenia, there are many banks and currency exchange offices, which are located in major cities and towns. If you are planning a long trip, for example, to mountains or remote villages, it is best to take care of currency exchange in advance. We also recommend exchanging bills of the local currency into smaller denominations, as in remote areas people live rather poorly, and maybe you will not even be able to exchange a 5000 AMD bill. The best option is always to have some coins and some amount of cash in denominations of 1000 AMD, and then you will definitely avoid trouble with the change at the shops or wherever.

When traveling to Armenia you can safely take cash in rubles, euros, and dollars. This is the most common currency in the country. Armenian Dram in the global foreign exchange market has a very low cost, and is highly dependent on the dollar and euro fluctuations.

Here is one of the most trustworthy websites –

www.rate.am, where you can not only keep track of the daily exchange rates in Armenia, but also make use of online converters. The website provides currency rates not only for global and common currencies but also for quite rare ones as for example the British pound, Swiss franc, Chinese yen, the Georgian lari, etc.

http://www.rate/en/armenian-dram-exchange-rates/banks/non-cash

Here you will find information on exchange rates in various banks and currency exchange offices, located inside supermarkets and large retail stores. The site contains information on the addresses and contact information of banks and exchange offices throughout Armenia.

There is a possibility of online conversion with the selected filters (bank, specific currency), and a quick search for the nearest to you banks or exchange offices.

In Armenia, currency exchange will not become a problem. Already on arrival at Zvartnots International airport you will be greeted by numerous branches of local banks. However, we do not recommend exchanging the entire amount at the airport, only the minimum necessary, in order to avoid unfavorable exchange rate. Also, do not exchange at the individual or street money changers not to be cheated.

Today, the number of banks and ATMs in Yerevan is steadily growing, and to find the right bank next to you is no trouble. Almost all the banks have international money transfer systems, such as the UNI Stream and MoneyGram, or sending and receiving currency through the SWIFT network. Visa, MasterCard or American Express credit cards are also becoming popular from year to year: most high-scale shops, restaurants, and hotels accept credit card payments.

However, before making a payment always pre-verify. Please note that outside of Yerevan making payments by credit card is almost impossible, so always carry local currency cash in small banknotes.

Prices in Armenia: Transport

As already stated in the «Public Transportation» chapter the most convenient way to move around Yerevan is by bus and minibus. Almost at any bus stop, you can take the necessary number and get to any part of the city. And the fare is surprisingly low: only 100 AMD ($0.2). There are also trolley-buses, which are not so many, but you can take them in case you wish to save money, as the fare is absolutely low – only 50 AMD ($0.1). By the way, there are no checks, conductors or tickets in these types of transport; you pay directly to the driver when taking off.

Prices in Armenia: Accommodation

The accommodation in Armenia cannot be considered the cheapest in the world, but not very expensive. The prices in the most luxurious hotels, such as Marriott, Tufenkian, Ani Plaza, Royal Tulip start from 50 000 AMD ($100) and higher.

Those who want to rent an apartment should take into consideration that the price depends on the location, number of rooms and quality of the repair. Accordingly, an apartment in the center of Yerevan with the good repair will not be cheaper than $ 180 per day. The farther from the center – the cheaper. The average price of renting an apartment in Yerevan is about 20,000 per day ($ 41).

Prices in Armenia: Products

Local products and local fruits and vegetables in Armenia are rather inexpensive. This is not surprising: Armenia is a sunny country with all the favourable climatic conditions for the cultivation of fruits and vegetables that are here in abundance.

If you are not going to stay in a hotel and will have to take care of your everyday menu, you can get familiar with the following prices:

Milk (regular) 1 liter

0,89$

Loaf of fresh white bread (500g)

0,49$

Rice (white) 1kg

1,18$

Eggs (12)

1,54$

Local cheese 1kg

4,71$

Yogurt

0,3-0,6$

Sugar 1kg

1$

Butter 1kg

Starting from 3,2$

Chicken breasts 1 kg

4,67$

Beef 1kg

6,56$

Apples 1kg

0,97$

Banana 1kg

1,36$

Tomato 1kg

0,73$

Potato 1kg

0,49$

Onion 1 kg

0,50$

Lettuce 1 head

0,32$

Water 1,5 liter bottle

0,48$

Bottle of wine (mid-range)

5,24$

Domestic beer 0,5liter bottle

0,88$

Imported beer 0,33 liter bottle

1,23$

Cigarettes 20 pack (Marlboro)

1,26$

If you do not wish to dine at home or want to try Armenian national dishes, there is a wide range of both luxury restaurants and cafes offering fast-food.

Basic dinner out for two in neighborhood pub

4697 AMD

Dinner for two at an Italian restaurant in the expat area including appetizers, main course, wine and dessert

20.475 AMD

1 cocktail drink in downtown club

2813 AMD

1 beer in neighbourhood pub (500ml or 1pt.)

817 AMD

Other

While traveling in Armenia you should allocate some budget to other traveling expenses, such as, telecommunication (unless you're using roaming of your local operator). You can buy SIM cards in any newspaper booth (providing your passport in some cases) for about AMD1000, and talk inside Armenia from AMD20-30 per minute. You can find more information about telecommunication operators and tariffs in the respective websites of the companies (Beeline

Armenia, VivaCell-MTS, Orange, U!com and Rostelecom) or their offices throughout the country.

To get a prepaid SIM card, visit one of the above carriers with your passport, and sign up; it should take about five minutes and cost 500 AMD. Most major international carriers also provide roaming services, which you should activate prior to arrival.

Internet and Wi-Fi is widely available throughout Yerevan, especially in cafes and hotels. Many parks also offer free Wi-Fi! Availability of Wi-Fi outside Yerevan is limited, but available at most major hotels.

USEFUL INFORMATION

INTERNATIONAL DIALING CODE FOR ARMENIA IS 374.

Emergency Contacts

1. Fire Department – 101

2. Police – 102

3. Ambulance – 103

4. Gas Emergency Service – 104

5. Emergency Situations Crisis Management Center - 911, 101

6. Municipality of Yerevan Hotline – 108

7. Ombudsman (Human Rights Defender) of Armenia Hotline – 118

Medication and Vaccinations

There are no obligatory immunizations required for

travelers visiting Armenia. Armenia's climate is generally pleasant and does not pose unusual health risks. Medical facilities vary in quality and breadth, with many qualified doctors and dentists running a variety of practices. There are registered pharmacies on virtually every corner in the center of Yerevan, carrying all of the basic toiletries and many over-the-counter drugs, some of which can also be purchased in hotels and supermarkets. If you have special health needs, speak to your physician before traveling. If you travel during the summer, it is a good idea to pack sunscreen, a hat and sunglasses, as the Armenian sun is strong!

Insurance

Even though Armenia is one of the safest countries to travel to, boasting one of the lowest crime rates worldwide, and ranking eighth on this year's Gallup Poll on how safe people feel, taking out a travel insurance policy that covers theft, loss, accidents and medical problems is highly recommended. If you plan to do any adventure or extreme sports such as scuba diving, bungee jumping, motorcycling, skiing and even hiking, check that your policy fully covers you.

More information on local insurance packages is available at:

1. Ingo Armenia

2. Nairi Insurance

3. Sil Insurance

4. Rosgosstrakh Armenia

5. Armenia Insurance

6. Reso Insurance

.   .   .

Postal Service

You can send and receive anything from postcards to large packages to and from anywhere in the world via HayPost, the Armenian post office. There are also logistics companies available. The following are the most widely used providers:

EMS Armenia Express Mail Service

UPS express

DHL Worldwide Express

Federal Express

TNT Express Worldwide

CITIES, VILLAGES AND PROVINCES WORTH VISITING

Armenia has several worthy cities, villages, and provinces to visit throughout the country. Here we go!

Yerevan

One of the most prominent peculiarities about the Armenian capital are the pinkish architecture, cafe culture, and the endless amounts of things to do in Yerevan. New bars and restaurants in Yerevan are constantly opening their doors but the refined charm still stays in place. To feel the endless energy of the city you need to have a walking tour in Yerevan. Walking around the city center is the simplest way to feel the energy and breath of the city.

Must Do Things in Yerevan

To feel the endless energy of the city you need to have a walking tour in Yerevan. Walking around the city center is the simplest way to feel the energy and breath of the city.

There are many amazing places to go in Yerevan which you can visit while traveling around the capital. The city will impress both lovers of cognitive tours and those who looking for entertainment and vivid emotions despite its ancient age. Wide variety of attractions will satisfy the needs of tourists with any preferences. The city is rich with history, culture, and hospitality. Yerevan is a city of museums and visiting some of them is a must do for everyone who wants to understand the rich history and culture of the country.

The main attractions of the Armenian capital are the **Matenadaran Institute of Ancient Manuscripts, the Erebuni Historical and Archaelogical Museum-Reserve** founded in the 8th century BC, **the History Museum of Armenia, Genocide Memorial and Museum, Sergei Parajanov museum**, art galleries, museums and other cultural places of Yerevan. The History museum was founded in 1931 and the current building (built in 2005) was designed by Jim Torosyan in a complex shared with the Yerevan City Hall. There are over 90,000 objects and artifacts at the museum that take visitors back all the way to ancient times. If you're a history enthusiast or simply want to learn more about Armenia's capital city, add this to your list of things to do in Yerevan! You can find the Yerevan History Museum at 1/1 Argishti Street in Yerevan.

Matenadaran Institute of Ancient Manuscripts

The Matenadaran is both a museum of ancient manuscripts and a scientific research institute. The collection of manuscripts of Matenadaran is one of the biggest in the world. The depository contains over 17300 manuscripts, 450 thousand archive documents, 3000 ancient books. Over 14200 manuscripts kept are in Armenian, the rest ones are in foreign languages – Greek, Latin, Aramaic, Hebrew, Arabic, Persian, Old Slavonic, Ethiopic, Japanese and others. Unique examples of translation are kept here, the origins of which weren't saved. You can find Matenadaran at Mashtots Avenue 53, for more information visit www.matenadaran.am.

Erebuni Historical and Archaelogical Museum-Reserve

This archaeological site dates from 782 BC, three decades before Rome was established. It gives an excellent insight into daily life in the palace of Argishti I, one of the greatest kings of Urartu. The first stage of excavations here started in 1950, after a farmer unearthed an inscribed stone tablet. Archaeologists swooped in and soon found a large cuneiform slab with the inscriptions of Argishti I confirming the date when the fortress was constructed. They went on to uncover the remains of courtyards, halls, temples and rooms that were part of the royal palace. Dozens of Urartian and Achaemenid artefacts and mural fragments were also found, many of which are now displayed in the museum. You can find the Museum at Erebuni Street 38, for more information visit www.erebuni.am.

History Museum of Armenia

The main museum of Armenia is the National History Museum, located on the Republic Square. Examine a collection of 400,000 objects at History Museum of Armenia, displaying archaeological finds, ethnographic items, and historical relics. Established in 1920, the national museum preserves Armenia's cultural heritage across themed sections- numismatics, ethnography, archaeology, modern history, and restoration. The Museum of History of Armenia is a truly amazing treasury, moving along which one can literally feel the flow of time and travel through the ages. Here you can see historical documents, objects of ancient life, clothes, medieval weapons, chariots and a collection of coins that were in use in Armenia in different epochs. To make a real fascinating journey into the depths of centuries, it is worth ordering an excursion with a guide. You can find the Museum at Republic Square 4, for more information visit www.historymuseum.am.

Armenian Genocide Memorial & Museum

Commemorating the massacre of Armenians in the Ottoman Empire from 1915 to 1922, this institution offers a powerful museum experience similar to that of Israel's Yad Vashem (Holocaust Museum). The two-storey exhibition space is built into the side of the hill so as not to detract from the monument above. The story of this horrific historical event is told through photographs, documents, newspaper reports and films. The complex is on Tsitsernakaberd Hill (Fortress of Swallows) across the Hrazdan Gorge from central Yerevan. The easiest way to get here is via taxi (AMD800 to AMD1200 from the city centre). So you can find the Armenian Genocide Memorial and Museum at 8/8 Tsitsernakaberd highway. For more information visit www. genocide-museum.am.

Sergei Parajanov Museum

The Sergei Parajanov Museum is a tribute to Soviet Armenian director and artist Sergei Parajanov and is one of the most popular museums in Yerevan. It represents

Parajanov's diverse artistic and literary heritage. His films and artworks had a unique style. You can get familiar with his works at his Museum in Yerevan. The museum was founded in 1988 when Parajanov moved to Yerevan. Parajanov himself chose the place and construction project of museum. Due to the 1988 Armenian earthquake and socio-economic problems, the museum was opened only in June 1991, one year after Parajanov's death. You can find Sergei Parajanov Museum at Dzoragyugh 1st Street, for more information visit www.parajanovmuseum.am.

Cascade complex

Highly Recommended! Complete your first impression of the city at **Cascade Complex** and **Cafesjian Museum of Art** – it is a unique combination of beautiful view of the city and the Holy mountain Ararat plus modern art. Located in the famous Cascades complex in Yerevan, this contemporary museum of art extends from Tamanyan street up the Cascades. Having opened in 2009, the museum receives around one million visitors annually. The Cascades are a giant stairway in Yerevan made of limestone that was built in 1971 and completed in 1980.

There are fountains, statues, and a handful of cafes, bars, and restaurants in the area. Even though it may garner more tourists than other areas of the city, it is still one of my favorite places to go in Yerevan. The Cascades have an escalator inside for those unable to walk the stairs to the top. You can find the Cascades at 10 Tamanyan *Street* in Yerevan.

Ararat Brandy Factory

You can't leave Armenia without visiting **Ararat brandy factory**. This is what people call real Armenian flavor! Ararat is a famous brandy (marketed as cognac) that has been produced by the Yerevan Brandy Company since 1887. You can try the drink almost anywhere in Yerevan, or you can actually go to the Yerevan Brandy Factory itself and take a tour or visit the museum dedicated to the stuff. To find out more, check out their website https://en.araratbrandy.com. You can find the Yerevan Brandy Factory at 2 Admiral Isakov Avenue on the Hrazdan Gorge in Yerevan.

Vernisage Flea Market

Shop for local hand-made items! **Vernisage** flea market– this is a great place to snatch up a variety of traditional Armenian art work, such as rugs, wood carvings, paintings, musical instruments and jewelry. Visiting Vernisage is a full day free excursion which brings you one step closer to Armenian culture and traditions. Even if you leave the place with empty hands (which is hardly possible:) at least you will get a good handle on the country's culture. Weekend is the best time to visit Vernisage. Always bargain, as a higher price might be told to foreigners.

Blue Mosque

The Blue Mosque in Yerevan is an 18th-century Shia mosque located in the city center. During the Soviet-era, when religion was shunned, the mosque was used to house the History Museum of Yerevan. When Armenia became a free country, the Blue Mosque converted back into a mosque, which is used by the many Iranians living in Yerevan. It is the only mosque in Armenia today. Iran is the current owner of the mosque and will be for several decades into the future. You can find the Blue Mosque at 12 Mashtots Avenue in Yerevan.

Yerevan Opera Theatre

The Yerevan Opera Theatre opened its doors in 1933 and has been a main point of interest in Yerevan since. Designed by architect Alexander Tamanian, the Opera building has two halls, the Aram Khatchaturian hall and the Alexander Spendiaryan Opera and Ballet National Theatre, seating 1,400 people and 1,200 people, respectively. There are a lot of children's games, rides, and other events happening outsite. Visiting it is definitely one of the most common things to do in Yerevan. You can find the Yerevan Opera Theatre at 54 Tumanyan Street in Yerevan.

The Gum Market

Want to immerse into the local culture? Then Gum market is the right place for you to feel the Armenian hospitality, openness and enjoying the original display of Armenian fresh and dried fruits.

The displays of fresh and dried fruits at this covered market are pretty as a picture, so it's fortunate that the stallholders don't seem to mind tourists photographing their wares. In summer, the fresh fruit is magnificent, with peaches, cherries, apricots and berries of every description tempting shoppers. In winter, dried fruits and nuts, including the strings of syrup-coated walnuts known as *sujukh*, are popular purchases. Other produce includes fresh vegetables, aromatic herbs, pungent *basturma* (finely cured ham) and huge blocks of cheese.

Day-trips from Yerevan

Yerevan is situated in a convenient area for a handful of day trips. Here are some recommended day trips from Yerevan and other places to visit in Armenia.

Temple of Garni

The Temple of Garni is an Ionic temple located in Garni, Armenia and is the only colonnaded building in Armenia and the former USSR. It represents pre-Christian Armenia and was likely built in the first century AD. The Temple of Garni is often visited together with Geghard Monastery and it receives over 200,000 visitors annually.

The only one of its kind, the temple of Garni has become the symbol of pre-Christian Armenia and is located forty-five minutes from Yerevan in the temple's namesake village. History and culture lovers will enjoy seeing this vestige of the Roman Empire all the way east into Armenia. The views of the nearby valley are beautiful, and the drive from Yerevan is lush and scenic.

Today, the Temple of Garni is one of the most popular tourist sites in Armenia and serves as the central shrine for Armenian Neopaganism.

Geghard Monastery

Geghard Monastery is a popular day trip from Yerevan. Geghard Monastery was inscribed into the UNESCO World Heritage List in 2000 and is one of only four such sites in the country. Geghard represents the peak of medieval Armenian architectural achievement and comprises a walled complex set in stunning mountain scenery in the upper Azat Valley in Kotayk Province.

UNESCO describes the site as being an exceptionally complete and well-preserved example of a medieval Armenian monastic foundation. Geghard was founded in the 4th century, according to tradition by St. Gregory the Illuminator.

Like many important Christian sites, Geghard was built in a place that was already a Hellenic pilgrimage site. Visitors today do more than just tour the building; they take place in this ancient pilgrimage rituals by drinking or dousing themselves in water that comes into the monastery via a holy spring.

. . .

Khor Virap

In a country with some hundred or so monasteries, you'd be forgiven for thinking that after a while, they all look the same. Not so for Khor Virap, one of the most scenic monasteries in all of Armenia. Located about 45 minutes outside of Yerevan, Khor Virap is perhaps best known for its stunning backdrop of Mount Ararat, historically part of Armenia but later annexed by Turkey. Due to its location nearby the (closed) Turkish border, Khor Virap has one of the best views you can get of Mount Ararat within Armenia.

Khor Virap means "deep dungeon" and according to legend, Saint Gregory the Illuminator was imprisoned here in the 3rd century for 13 years. After his imprisonment, he succeeded in converting Armenia into a Christian nation and becoming head of the Armenian Apostolic Church. Pope Francis visited the monastery in 2016.

Lake Sevan

Sevan is a must visit destination when exploring and touring around Armenia. Lake Sevan is one of the star attractions and an incredibly popular destination for Armenians. It's also home to the Sevanavank, a monastery, and church that was built in the 9th century. There is so much to do at Lake Sevan, not only can you beat the heat in the summertime, it's beautiful all year round. Popular activities in the area include all kinds of water sports like swimming, surfing or skiing. Delicious fish dinners are a must when visiting the lake also.

Set 1900m above sea level, the great blue expanse of Sevana Lich (Lake Sevan) covers 940 sq km, and is 80km long by 30km at its widest. The largest lake in the Caucasus, it's also one of the largest freshwater high-altitude lakes in the world.

Its colours and shades change with the weather and by its own mysterious processes, from a dazzling azure to dark blue and a thousand shades in between.

The lake supports a healthy fish population, including the endangered ishkhan (prince trout), named for a row of spots like a crown on its head. Other species include introduced crayfish and sig (white fish).

Tsakhkadzor

If you've already in Armenia and like to spend your leisure time in nature, breathe some fresh air and see beautiful places, Tsakhkadzor is always a good idea for you and your friends. By the way, the city is not far from Yerevan, it is located at 2-hour ride from the capital of Armenia.

The top list of things to do in this paradise opens the beautiful church in Tsaghkadzor called "Kecharis", a medieval monastery complex which was built in the early-mid ages nearly in the 1050s. During centuries this place was ruled by different Armenian royal families, it was even conquered by Turks but then it was taken back by Armenians.

You can't visit Tsaghkadzor and don't have a little adventure on a cable car. It's no matter which season. A fantastic view and emotions are provided. It's a good possibility to see the beauty of the Armenian nature.

There are so many entertainment centers in Tsaghkadzor - cafes, casinos, restaurants, pubs. So if you want to relax and pass a nice time in the evening, you have a big variety of choice. Famous Kalyan Lounge, Royale Entertainment Center, Parisian Casino and not only.

The perfect time to visit Tsaghkadzor is winter which is a great place not only for beginners also for professionals to skate, both on snowboarding and on skies. For winter active sports lovers the weather in Tsaghkadzor is fantastic. Professional athletes from all over the world come here for sports camps. Everyone who visited here will claim that tracks are simply gorgeous.

Carahunge

Carahunge is a prehistoric archaeological site that many foreigners refer to as the Armenian Stonehenge. The vertical basalt stones are scattered across an open area and cover approximately 70 square kilometres (43.5 square miles). Archaeological explorations have shown that it is likely the area was used as an observatory and is at least 3,500 years older than Stonehenge.

It is located on a plateau that is 1770 meters above sea level. The complex occupies a territory of seven hectares- for comparison, it occupies as much territory as fourteen football fields together.

· · ·

Armenian Alphabet Monument

Visiting the Armenian Alphabet Monument is one of the more awesome things to do in the country. Just a 50-minute drive from the city, these 39 giant stone letters were installed in 2005 to commemorate the 1,600th birthday of the Armenian alphabet. The area was chosen carefully, as it's the final resting place of Mesrop Mashtots who is credited with creating the alphabet.

This place is not just an architectural creation, but a real tourist attraction where you can admire the elegant forms of the letters of the Armenian alphabet, find your initials and take a picture on their background for a memory.

Just above the complex is the 33-meter-high Holy Cross, symbolizing the age of the crucifixion of Jesus Christ. It consists of 1711 large and small metal crosses, which symbolize the age of Christian Armenia. The Cross is placed on the chapel, which is 301 cm. The number 301 symbolizes the date of adoption of Christianity in Armenia. During the construction it was planned that one more cross will be installed on the Cross every year.

Saghmosavank Monastery (The Monastery of Psalms)

The Armenian Apostolic Monastery complex Saghmosavank is located in the village of Sagmosavan of the Aragatsotn province of the Republic of Armenia. Prince Vache Vachutyan and his family built the complex in the 13th century.

Saghmosavank was a significant center for quality scholarship and calligraphy, with an established medieval higher structure of schooling. A constant rivalry among the monasteries of Saghmosavank and Hovhannavank raged for the title of the most beautiful of all the churches in the province. To decide which of the two deserves the title, one must visit them both!

The roof structure of the narthex of the Sagmosavank church is one of the exceptional examples in Armenian architecture. Unique decorations of the narthex are a pair of large windows on the southern facade and a western entrance, framed with an amazing horseshoe-shaped arch.

Hovhannavank Monastery

Hovhannavank Monastery majestically rises above a steep cliff. It is a unique historical monument built in the Middle Ages due to its size and complex architectural structure. The monastery was founded by the first Catholicos of Armenia Gregory the Illuminator who buried in this place the relics of John (Hovhannes) the Baptist and "Hovhannavank" is derived from his name. Distinctive feature of Hovhannavank is the compact arrangement of structures around the dominant building. The walls of the monastery are decorated with relief ornaments and inscriptions.

There were various educational institutions, a secondary school in the monastery, where philosophy, music, philology was taught. In Hovanavank there worked dozens of copyists who copied many manuscripts. Nowadays, there are about 20 manuscripts preserved in The Mesrop Mashtots Institute of Ancient Manuscripts – Matenadaran, which is located in Yerevan.

Byurakan Observatory

If you want to visit a place with a beautiful view of Mount Aragats Byurakan may be one of the best choices for you. The village is on the slope of the mountain in Argatsotn Province.

Byurakan Observatory is a great day trip for those who love space. Built during Soviet times, Byurakan served as Armenia's premier astronomical centre. Back in the day, it housed the largest telescope in the USSR and played an important part in bringing the country into the modern scientific field.

In Byurakan Observatory more than 1000 flare starts, several dozens of Supernovae, and hundreds of galaxies were discovered. Currently, the observatory is owned and operated by Armenian Academy of Science.

Although no new researches are done in the observatory, it is still active. The entrance fee for Armenians is 1000 AMD and for foreigners 1600 AMD. By visiting there, you will have an opportunity to observe the moon, planets and beautiful stars.

Areni Caves

For those interested in human history, there is no better place in Armenia than the Areni caves.

Home one of the oldest known wineries in the world, the earliest known leather shoe, one of the oldest surviving brains, and a 6,000-year-old straw skirt (talk about well-made clothing), this cave complex offers a fascinating look into the lives of people during the Bronze Age. Digging began in 2007 and continues to this day.

. . .

Noravank Monastery

Noravank is located in central Vayots Dzor Province, roughly 75 miles southeast of Yerevan in the Amaghu Valley. The monastery complex Noravank was built in the 13th-14th centuries. The complex consists of two churches and a chapel. Most noteworthy is the two-story Surb Astvatsatsin (Holy Mother of God) church, with its extravagant carvings. The architect Siranes (at the end of the XII century) and the outstanding sculptor and miniaturist Momik (XIV) worked here.

They say that master Momik fell in love with Prince Orbelian's beautiful daughter. The beauty also liked the talented architect. The girl's father, hearing about that, asked Momik to visit him and said: "I will let you marry my daughter, but only if you build for me a temple of incredible beauty in less than three years." The young master accepted the price's requirements and immediately started to work. When he, sitting at the very top of the temple's dome, put the last stone, suddenly a servant, sent by the prince, approached Momik and pushed him. Momik, trying to escape, grasped the last processed stone of the dome. Nevertheless, he fell to the ground and this stone became his tombstone.

Tatev Monastery and Wings of Tatev

Armenia has its fair share of provincial monasteries, but Tatev is an incredibly special one to visit. Built in the 9th century and later serving as both a monastery and a university, the Tatev complex is one of the most historically significant places to visit in Armenia. The historic Tatev Monastery is a 4.5-hour drive from Yerevan. However, the beautiful, misty mountainside complex, the ancient structures of the monastery, and the stunning views make the long trek worthwhile.

Tatev monastery in Armenia has its own "Wings". That is the longest reversible aerial tramway in the world – Wings of Tatev. The record was fixed in the Guinness Book on 16th of October, 2010, when the cable car opened its doors for the first visitors. The aerial tramway is 5752 meters long and "flies" up to 360 meters over the ground. Taking such "wings" you can reach the famous medieval monastery complex Tatev in only 12 minutes. It's around 4 times faster than it could take to the most comfortable car to go down and up the deep gorge between Halidzor village and the monastery on the other side of the canyon.

By visiting Tatev Monastery you not only will get acquainted with Armenian medieval architecture and see the unique man-made constructions but also experience the natural wonders such as so-called Devil's Bridge. It is created by wind, water, and salty soils, and hides a cave with an amazing lake, where you can swim if you'll dare. For not so courageous ones it could be easier, of course, to try the natural baths of hot springs of a different temperature that are located on the different height inside the caves and cliffs.

. . .

Stepanavan Dendropark

Stepanavan Dendropark is a natural forest, which has become a preserved park, including almost as much ornamental trees, as the wild forest trees are there. General surface covered by the park is 32.5 hectares, 17.5 ha of which is the natural forest and 15 ha – the ornamental trees. This is the biggest botanical garden in Armenia and the best place to explore Armenian nature in all its beauty and diversity.

This place is of great interest not only for nature and ecotourism lovers but also for the scientists. They can study here the rich biodiversity of Armenia. The collection of plants represents a great scientific development of species in uncommon climatic conditions. The plant collection is being maintained and is always expanding here. Moreover, Dendropark by itself makes room to study developmental changes in the plants.

This district is a pleasant and peaceful place for the excursions all year round with your family or friends. The garden is charming in every season.

Dilijan National Park

Dilijan national park's area is one of the unique corners in the Armenian nature, which distinguishes with its richness, rare diversity, meadow-forests landscapes, separate eco-systems with high economic values and natural monuments' protective, scientific-cognitive, medical and recreational high values. The park is located in the northern part of Armenia. The total area of Dilijan national park is 33765 ha which is divided into three zones; reserve, economic and recreation.

Besides the plants, Dilijan national park has rich fauna. Over 40 species of mammals such as brown bear, fox, lynx, red deer, roe, wild boar, wild cat, wolf, squirrel, badger, and others.

In the area of the reserve is located **Haghartsin** regarded as a school of architecture dating back many generations. It's because the refectory of Haghartsin monastery is the biggest in Armenia. It was an innovation of its time. Haghartsin Monastery rises among the majestic mountains where eagles fly and the name of temple is associated with them: Haghartsin in Armenian means "game of eagles". The symbol of this noble bird is also used in the architectural elements of the monastery.

Yell Extreme Park, Yenoqavan

Yell Extreme Park is located in Yenoqavan village, Tavush region. It is the most famous village among people who want to do extreme sports and those who want to have fun with friends and families. The key thing is not that you should be a professional sportsman, you can be part of these events without having special skills. The team of Extreme park professionals will help you to achieve your dreams.

Yell Extreme park is first of all, famous for Zipline, where the first zip-line flight took place in July 2015. It is designed to enable a user propelled by gravity to travel from the top to the bottom of the inclined cable by holding on to, or attaching to the freely moving pulley. ZipLine has 5 different lines: 135m, 268m, 200m, 375m, and 750m. The height is approximately 200-300 m above the ground. The average duration of the trip is 1.5h: 15 min for specialized training about the safety rules, from 30 secs to 2 min for each ZipLine depending on people's weight and 5-20 min walking after each flight to get from one line to another.

Lastiver

Located in Tavush, the Lastiver district is a paradise on earth! It's a place where you can escape from the hot heat and the city noise, a place where no one will be able to disturb your leisure.

Lastiver is within a few hours' drive from Yerevan and is one of the most favorite places for active leisure, both among the citizens of the country and the tourists.

While the road to Lastiver is gorgeous on its own, the beauty of Lastiver itself is hard to put into words. Here you will find wooden gazebos and lodges where you can spend the night at an additional cost. The houses are quite comfortable and will make you feel as if you're in one of your favorite fairy tales. On the territory of Lastiver there is also a bar and usually a large bonfire, around which people gather in the evening, play the guitar and sing their favorite songs in the company of one another. Locals are always happy to see people visiting and will greet you there with great hospitality.

Away from the wooden structures you will have a beautiful view of the waterfall. The water in the river is crystal clear - you can even drink it. But, keep in mind that it is very cold, so you cannot stay barefoot in it for long. However, this doesn't stop some daredevils who dive headfirst into the freezing cold spring water, an excellent way to boost their immune system.

. . .

Gyumri

"If you want to know Armenia, you must come to Gyumri", is a statement profoundly believed by all citizens of Shirak's capital town.

Sitting in the north western region of the country in the central Shirak Highland is Armenia's second largest city of Gyumri. It is situated around 126 kilometers away from the capital city of Yerevan.

While most of the people visiting Yerevan go for a day trip to one of the spectacular monasteries around the country Gyumri, the second biggest city in Armenia is also an interesting option. In ancient times, it was a trade crossroad for many different nations. It is home to some prominent museums, lovely parks and the impressive Kumayri historic district. Many may not realize this, but there is quite a lot to do in the city.

One of the landmarks of Gyumri is the monument to the legendary Vardan Mamikonyan, the hero of Armenia and the defender of the Christian religion, who is ranked among the saints. The Alexandropol fortress is another historical monument built to protect Russian borders from attacks by Turkish or Persian troops. Gyumri is considered a center of art and culture. The city is also called the "capital of humor" as it was here that many legendary artists and humorists of Armenia were born.

Charles Aznavour, Martiros Saryan, Aram Khachatryan and others are among Honorable citizens of Gyumri.

. . .

Etchmiadzin

Many guests often ask guides about the difference between Armenian Apostolic church and all the other Christian churches around the world. As stated above Armenia is the first country in the world to adopt Christianity as a state religion in 301 AD.

Tour to Holy Etchmiadzin will give you a chance to get acquainted with the peculiarities of Armenian Christianity, it's rich history and heritage. Etchmiadzin is a small town not so far from Yerevan – 15 km, where the mother church of the Armenian Apostolic Church – Etchmiadzin Cathedral is located. This town occupies a great place in the life of Armenian people, as exactly here began the development of original Armenian culture, exactly this town is considered the heart of Armenian Christianity and exactly here is situated the majestic Echmiadzin Cathedral and the Residence of Catholicos of all Armenians.In Etchmiadzin one can find numerous old churches, museums, the residence of the Supreme Patriarch and Catholicos of All Armenians and many other Christian facilities. Echmiadzin is often called "Armenian Vatican". It is also recommended to visit Etchmiadzin in days of Feasts of Jesus Christ and on the days of liturgies.

Jermuk

Jermuk is one of the most popular spa towns in Armenia because of its healing mineral waters and mild climate. The town has more than 40 thermal springs! In Jermuk, you can visit the Gallery of Water for free tastings of the healing mineral waters. And don't forget to visit the most popular attraction – Jermuk Waterfall, which is the second largest waterfall in Armenia. The water tumbles down from the height of about 70m. This day tour from Yerevan brings you to five spectacular sites including Jermuk Waterfall.

Artsakh

Basic facts about Artsakh

Currency: Armenian Dram (AMD)

Language: A dialect of Armenian is the most widely spoken language. Most people speak Russian but very little English.

Population: 150,000

Capital: Stepanakert

Drinking Water: The water is safe to drink in most towns in Artsakh. Check with your hosts first.

Wi-Fi: Many places will claim to have Wi-Fi. It usually works enough to send an email or receive messages but don't plan on uploading pictures or watching movies.

ARTSAKH

A SPECIAL CHAPTER SHOULD BE DEDICATED TO ARTSAKH. FOR centuries this land, on the fringe of the oldest Christian civilization, has defended its faith and independence.

Unique traditions, magic nature, rich cultural heritage and local cuisine make Artsakh very attractive for tourists. Necessary touristic infrastructures are developed here for guest's comfort. Within the short period of this tour you will have the opportunity of being acquainted with both rich cultural and historic heritage and Artsakh people, their customs, traditions, legends and famous cuisine.

Despite the fact that Artsakh borders with three countries - the Republic of Armenia, the Republic of Azerbaijan and the Islamic Republic of Iran - for tourists, still the main route to Artsakh passes through Armenia. Quite attractive route of approximately 350 km - the main highway connecting Yerevan to Stepanakert - passes through the northern regions of Armenia, the cities of Yeghegnadzor, Vayk, Goris. The main highway is in good condition and works year round. Duration, depending on the vehicle, runs in the range of 4 to 6 hours. Every day, from 8:00 am with an interval of 1 hour from the Central bus station in Yerevan the buses and minibuses travel to Stepanakert, arriving in for 5-6 hours. Ticket price is 5,000 drams (about 10 USD). Also, from the station, travelers can hire four-seated cab. The fare for a taxi to Stepanakert is about 18 USD per passenger.

For entry to the territory of Artsakh Republic foreign citizens must have a valid passport or other identification document, the AR entry visa. Entry visa (permission) of the Artsakh Republic may be obtained in the AR representation in Armenia, as well as in Stepanakert in the AR Ministry of Foreign Affairs. Free 21-day tourist visa of the Artsakh Republic may be obtained at border points upon entry to country.

Today, Nagorno-Karabakh (Artsakh) is a de facto independent state with its capital Stepanakert and the cultural center Shushi. The rich history of this region dates back many centuries, and historical and architectural sights, which can be found everywhere, even under the open sky, testify that.

Here are top sightseeing places of Artsakh which you should definitely include in your tour program.

Stepanakert

The capital city of Artsakh was not what we were expecting at all. The main street and some of the surrounding buildings have been recently renovated and fashion boutiques, up-market hotels and cafes slowly give way to derelict buildings and empty lots as you walk further from the centre. The main streets and squares are busy with people shopping, chatting and watching children dash around on scooters.

There's a good selection of bars and restaurants, a museum and even some street art to be found. A day is enough time to explore the sights of Stepanakert.

Shushi/Shusha

Shushi is a small town about 12km from Stepanakert. It has been through a lot of conflict and as a result the population has been greatly diminished. Nevertheless, the town is very sweet and there is plenty of history and nature to discover. Shushi is museum capital and you can find five different museums with a 20 minute walk. The town also has ancient walls and a short walk takes you to a viewpoint with incredible views down the Hunot Canyon.

The monument "We Are Our Mountains"

The monument "We are our Mountains", located at the entrance to Stepanakert is one of the main and recognizable symbols and attractions of Artsakh (Nagorno-Karabakh). The image of the monument is presented on the coat of arms of the Republic of Artsakh, and among Armenians it is called gently "grandmother and grandfather" (in Armenian "tatik-papik").

Ancient fortresses

There are several well-preserved ancient fortresses, most of which are included in excursions and tours as sightseeing places. Among the most significant fortress buildings can be noted Tigranakert, Mayraberd, Shushi fortress and Kachaghakaberd.

. . .

Churches and monasteries

Among the most ancient monasteries of this region are Dadivank and Amaras. Amaras Monastery was founded in the IV century. The author of the Armenian alphabet, Mesrop Mashtots, founded here the very first school of Nagorno-Karabakh in the V century. Another beautiful monument of Armenian architecture is the 12th century monastery of Gandzasar: the name literally means "Treasure Mountain". It is impossible to ignore the later (1868-1887), but the fabulously beautiful snow-white Cathedral of Surb Amenaprkich Ghazanchetsots (Cathedral of Saint Christ the Savior).

Hunot Gorge

Hunot Gorge is a stunning and beautiful sight of untouched wild nature, surrounded by a picturesque mountain landscape. A clean mountain river flows at the bottom of the canyon; you can even swim in the cool water. Fans of active tourism often take tents and organize camping in Hunot Gorge during warm season in order to admire beautiful natural views at different times of the day.

Jermajur

Jermajur, one of the most popular sightseeing places, is a high-mountainous region of healing hot springs, located at an altitude of 2,200 meters above sea level. The name "Jermajur" is translated from Armenian as "hot water".

. . .

Waterfall "Umbrella"

Waterfall "Umbrella" is an unusual and very popular natural landmark. The name of the waterfall comes from its shape, which really resembles an umbrella with streams of rainwater flowing continuously from it.

The Skhtorashen plane tree (Tnjri)

Approximately 37 km from Stepanakert, near the village of Skhtorashen, you can see a unique, giant tree – the Skhtorashen plane tree (Tnjri). Tnjri is the oldest (2035 years old) and the tallest (over 54 m) tree in the CIS. There is a hollow at the base of the green giant, inside of which 100 people can simultaneously accommodate. The area covered by the foliage of the tree is 1400 sq.m.

Paragliding

Paragliding in Armenia has developed in the past few years. In recent years, many professional pilots visit here paragliding and exploring new flying destinations. Because this land is a very attractive destination for para-tourism due to 300 sunny days a year and convenient weather conditions for both independent and tandem flights.

The flights usually take place in Mt Hatis, Aparan, Lake

Sevan, Buzhakan, and Dilijan. Flying above Sevan Lake is a great experience that everyone should try. During your flight, you will be the witness of something special, the huge marvelous lake framed with the mountain range and the blue sky. All of these create a view that you will never forget. When you are in the air, you feel yourself as a bird in the sky, the emotions, feelings, adrenaline and the beauty around give your life experience. Right after the launch, you want to fly again.

The duration of the flight lasts from 7 minutes to 15-20 depending on the weather conditions. The flights with an instructor costs 1 participant 48.000 AMD (83 EUR/ 99 USD), 3-5 participants 43.000 AMD (74 EUR / 88 USD), 6 and more participants 40.000 AMD (69 EUR / 82 USD).

This is lifetime adventure that can be done in the heights of Armenian highlands, do not lose this opportunity when you visit the land of miracles.

Rock climbing

The mountains have been another proud of Armenia, and this is not surprising that their national symbol is the biblical mountain Ararat, though it is not in the area of the country.

Armenia has the Federation of Rock climbing which organizes different competitions and open championships.

The most developed area for climbing is the Noravank Canyon. It is located on the main road Yerevan-Goris. The climbing track attracts many climbers with its heights and difficulty. Some say that Armenia has the best climbing track area in the world. Besides their sport, climbers will be able to see the marvelous nature of Yeghegnadzor, see one of the famous churches in Armenia, called Noravank.

The other extraordinary place for climbers is located in Garni's gorge 23km east of Yerevan, called "The symphony of stones". It is considered to be a natural monument which is included in the list of natural monuments of Armenia. The symphony seems to be artificial rocks sorted one by one. Actually, these stones were created under high pressure, in the result of volcanic lava's freezing and crystallization.

Year by year the number of rock climbers and sports amateurs rises up.

Hiking

Armenia is heaven for those who are ready for active tours full of discoveries and adventures. There are lots of tours that organize hiking tours in the area of Armenia and Nagorno Karabakh. During the tour, you will be able to see the treasures of Armenian Nature and the heights of Armenian uplands.

One of the popular hiking places is Aragats Mountain (4090). It is the highest peak in Armenia, an extinct volcano which has four peaks. The Southern peak of Aragats is for non-professional climbers, but if you are professional the Northern peak is more convenient for you because it requires serious preparedness. For climbing the mountain, the most suitable months are June and August that time of the year the trails are dry. But this mountain becomes a perfect place for professional climbers in winters.

Mountain Khustup is another beautiful place for hikers which is located in Syunik Province. This mountain is not high (3200) but for reaching to the top of it the hikers should walk 3-4 days, change the valleys and then should find the secret path which leads to the mountain Khustup. The hikers call this Mountain 3D model made by designers because it isn't as easy to climb as it seems. Come and visit this mysterious place, enjoy the picturesque view of this marvelous Mountain.

Riding

If you planned to visit Armenia for new adventures and experiences, know that this little country is a just perfect place for you. Armenians started to get along with horses still in pagan times, these loyal animals were the inseparable part of any rituals and events. That means these people know how to treat and communicate with the extremely loyal and smart animals. So that without a doubt horse-riding will be another great way of passing your active rest and getting the enjoyable memories from the sunny country.

The most famous horse-racing centers are Hovik Hayrapetyan Equestrian Center, "10out of 10" complex, Ayrudzi Riding Club and many other companies that organize horse-riding tours out of Yerevan. All the riding lovers can enjoy their day in those centers. You will be able to feed the horses and participate in the process of saddling and ride horses.

Winter sports

You want to do sports, eat well and be invited as guests to many unknown Armenian people and be treated many tasty national dishes? Snowy Armenia waits for you. Armenia has two opposite weather conditions too hot summer and too cold winter (not usually but happens). So that dry and hot summers are being followed by cold and chilly winters but it is not a reason for tourists not to visit this wonderful country. Armenia has a lot of activities for winter sports lovers and amateurs.

The most visited destination in cold weather remains marvelous Tsaghkadzor. It is one of the three resort towns of Armenia and a place which all the locals love and prefer to visit.

If you are a free rider you can ski on the slopes of Mount Aragats, which is also a great place for professional climbers and winter sports lovers. The other Mountains Ara and Hatis are also convenient for mountain climbing. If you are a risk taker and ready for new challenges, this sport is for you. Armenian Mountains will give you the opportunity to try one of the best experiences in your life.

Off Road Driving

The land of miracles is considered to be a mountainous and stony country which makes perfect conditions for off-roading. Recently, off-road tours became very popular amongst extreme lovers and sports amateurs. Mountain roads on the edges of huge canyons, wonderful landscapes of Armenia make good conditions for a good ride.

Off-road or Jeeping tours are a perfect type activity that all the active rest lovers. They are served by experienced drivers with many years of practice. But if you want you can drive the car yourself (under the direction of instructor). During your tour, the dose of adrenaline, the impassable mountain roads and wonderful landscapes of Armenia will give you the indescribable feelings and memories.

Camping

Yes, Armenia is a paradise for camping, the people are hospitable, generous and you can easily forget that you decided to camp out and be invited for a dinner or a night at home without paying money. Apart from mountains, Armenia is rich with forests and valleys with rivers and natural springs which make wonderful preconditions for camping. If you want to change your style of resting, you want to change the boring and identical hotels and prefer the wildlife of this country offers you the best "wild" experience.

www.ingramcontent.com/pod-product-compliance
Lightning Source LLC
LaVergne TN
LVHW041337200726
843509LV00009B/746